GOD HEALED ME

24 HEALING SCRIPTURE VERSES AND PROMISES THAT HELPED ME RECOVER. BLACK & WHITE EDITION

in gratitude composed by MIMI EMMANUEL for MOSAIC HOUSE CO

GOD Healed Me.

Another Mosaic House publication. Sola Scriptura for Lovers of the Word, non-denominational.

We use the King James Bible and also occasionally Young's Literal Translation as mentioned.

Contact details www.mosaichouse.co, PB 25 Noosa, Qld 4567, Australia

Cover and interior design: Mimi, Pearl and sunnyEdesign
Editor: Elaine Roughton
Printer: CreateSpace

DEDICATION

This book is dedicated to those who are in need of any kind of healing.

It is my sincere wish and prayer that you may find health and healing and the peace and joy that comes from the knowledge that GOD is always in charge.

RECEIVE MY NEXT BOOK FOR FREE

GOD HEALED ME is the first in a series of twelve about God's mercy, miracles and promises.

Coming up are 'LIVE FOREVER HOW TO and as an aside, 'THE HOLY GRAIL OF BOOK LAUNCHING.'

If you like to receive a copy of my next book for FREE, you can sign up to Mimi's book releases here http://eepurl.com/bHUzf5

FREE SCRIPTURE DESIGNS

I like you to benefit as much from GOD's Holy Word as I do and for this reason I have included a link to 24 free downloadable Scripture printables. These Scripture verses are the same designs as you find in this book and you can print these verses up from your own home printer.
You will find this link under Promos and Freebies.

CONTENTS

FOREWORD

It is my complete pleasure and honor to recommend Mimi and her work to a wider audience.

Although Mimi and I live at completely opposite ends of this planet, our weekly discussions on life, writing and the universe are a real highlight of my week.

I have learnt three really important things about Mimi.

Mimi is a great Accountability Buddy. She understands the 'ups and downs' of life'. So when we talk and I am down, she cheers me up and lifts me up.

Mimi is a good book coach. She knows as much as anyone does about how to write and launch books - great for me.

Mimi is a really wise friend. Mimi not only understands the Bible, but has lived through all the verses she writes about. Not just lived through - perhaps 'pushed through' would be a better phrase. The wisdom that comes from experience shines through. This is why Mimi's writing is worth reading.

This book - I am delighted to say - is one of twelve. All full of Mimi's wisdom and love. I suggest you read it all once (treat yourself) and then come back, and read one section per day from then on - that's what I'm doing. Choose randomly, but I am sure our Lord will point you to what you need to read each day.

In one of our conversations, Mimi described a parrot that had befriended her and her daughters - it came to live with them. She had decided to call the parrot 'Mercy' - which I think was very prophetic.

Once, when I was in Uganda preaching on Psalm 23, I found myself translating verse six, as follows... 'Surely the only things really pursuing me, are God's goodness and mercy'. This might not be an accurate translation, but it does, I believe reflect what David, felt when he was pursued by his enemies.

I thought of this verse when Mimi told me about her parrot, Mercy.

My prayer for Mimi - and you dear reader is the same - may 'God's goodness and mercy pursue you/live with you/keep hold of you all the days of your life'.

And may you read all of Mimi's books.
Blessings

Ian Banner
Author of HOW TO HEAR GOD
https://amzn.com/B005OTK8BS

HOW TO READ THIS BOOK

How should you read and use this book? You can read this book as you would with any other book you pick up, from front to back.

Or you can read this book by finding and reading the Scripture verses that apply to your life right now, and use these verses to uplift your spirit and as inspiration for a better life, a life filled with hope and encouragement. Better still, a life filled with promises from the Bible, promises that come true.

How do I know that these promises come true? Moses said so, as did Jesus, and in my own life my prayers are answered all the time. And this happened when I did not even know how to pray.

Initially all I said was, *'Father, help me please, thank you for hearing my prayers,'* and my prayers were answered. When I prayed for money, it arrived, when I prayed for comfort, I was comforted, when I prayed for understanding I received it.

Later on I learned that there is a formula for successful prayer.

What is our part in a 'Successful Prayer Formula?'
For our prayers to be answered, we have to play our part. I address this on my WordPress blog when I discuss Scripture card 'K'. See NOTES.

Various situations and Scripture verses all throughout the Bible tell us to trust, commit, call, seek, and ask humbly. We're told to do good and call upon Him in truth with all our heart. If necessary return to Him, if possible be in agreement with your nearest and dearest. Keep His words and commandments and ask according to His will. We're told to pray and to believe. In addition to what Jesus' prayer tells us, there is a minimum of three steps to the 'Successful Prayer Formula.'

K

Knock and it shall be
opened unto you.

(Matthew 7:7)

SUCCESSFUL PRAYER FORMULA

1. Be humble and bold.
2. Call in truth and faith.
3. Ask according to His will; trust and believe.

Sometimes a simple 'SOS' gets answered quickly. But ordinarily you can expect that there are two sides to having prayers answered, and you will have to play your part.

And now I will be sharing with you the words that so powerfully transformed my life.

I pray that these Scripture verses will do the same for you.

TRUST IN THE POWER OF PRAYER

With **GOD** *nothing shall be impossible.*

LUKE 1:37

PREFACE

PRAYER WORKS!

I've discovered that with God all things are possible, and that with God nothing shall be impossible.

I've known all my life that there is a God and I've known all my life that there is a heaven. What I wasn't well acquainted with was the Bible.

It wasn't until I was well in my forties that I started to read the Bible front to back. When I discovered the power of God's Holy Word, I fell head over heels and made many Scripture cards to have handy for when my spirit was low and I needed encouragement.

One of the first cards I made was with the Scripture verse, 'Ask and it shall be given you; seek and ye shall find...' This was one of the first cards I made because I had such an incredible experience when I prayed this prayer. Within a day of reciting this Scripture verse, I received a cheque for $15,000. (See NOTES.)

> From my WordPress blog: *"I prayed for treatment that would get me back on my feet. I figured at the time that I needed $15,000 to get me back up and running, as well as get some of my creditors of my back.*
>
> *I said, 'LORD, I know that with you all things are possible, and I need around $15,000, and I need it right now.' The next day I received a message that a completely unexpected $15,000 cheque was being written in my name. Within days that cheque was in the mail, and I was able to obtain the care I needed at the time and take some of the pressure off the financial woes and worries I was experiencing... This is a true story. Within one day of praying for $15,000 dollars I,*

completely unexpectedly and out of the blue, received that
exact amount when I reminded the LORD of what his SON told
his followers about the powers of GOD.

I rarely ever pray for money, but this time I did, and received a near enough instantaneous response.

In churches it is common to pray for a parishioner's health to improve, and now medical professionals such as cardiologist Randolph Byrd, Larry Dossey, M.D, members of Koenig of Duke University, and Dr. Matthews, associate professor of medicine at Georgetown University School of Medicine in Washington, D.C., all seem to agree that this may be a good idea.

THE POWER OF PRAYER

In the most widely publicized studies of the effect of intercessory prayer, cardiologist Randolph Byrd studied 393 patients admitted to the coronary-care unit at San Francisco General Hospital.

Some were prayed for by home-prayer groups, others were not. All the men and women got medical care.

In this randomized, double blind study, neither the doctors and nurses nor the patients knew who would be the object of prayer.

THE RESULTS WERE DRAMATIC AND SURPRISED MANY SCIENTISTS.

The men and women whose medical care was supplemented with prayer needed fewer drugs and spent less time on ventilators. They also fared better overall than their counterparts who received medical care but nothing more.

The prayed-for patients were:

- ✓ Significantly less likely to require antibiotics (3 patients versus 16)
- ✓ Significantly less likely to develop pulmonary edema, a condition in which the lungs fill with fluid because the heart cannot pump properly (6 versus 18).

14

✓ Significantly less likely to require insertion of a tube into the throat to assist breathing (0 versus 12).

NOTHING SEEMS TO BLOCK OR STOP THE EFFECTS OF PRAYER

In his 1994 book, "Healing Words," Larry Dossey, M.D., co-chair of the Panel on Mind-Body Interventions of the Office of Alternative Medicine at the National Institutes of Health in Washington, D.C., reviewed over 100 experiments, most published in parapsychological literature, on the effects of prayer/visualization. More than half showed an effect on everything from seed germination to wound healing.

The experiments showed that a simple "Thy will be done" approach was quantitatively more powerful than when specific results were held in mind.

A simple attitude of prayerfulness, an all-pervading sense of holiness, and a feeling of empathy, caring, and compassion for the entity in need seemed to set the stage for healing.

It did not matter whether the praying person was with the person who was prayed about for the power of prayer to work. You can pray for someone who is far away and still will have an influence on the outcome.

Nothing seems to block or stop the effects of prayer. The object in one study was placed in a lead-lined room and in another in a cage that shielded it from all known forms of electromagnetic energy; the effect still got through.

RESEARCH FROM KOENIG OF DUKE UNIVERSITY

"Studies have shown prayer can prevent people from getting sick, and when they do get sick, prayer can help them get better faster," says Duke University's Harold G. Koenig, M.D.

An exhaustive analysis of more than 1,500 reputable medical studies "indicates people who are more religious and pray more have better mental and physical health," Dr. Koenig says.

According to Dr. Koenig of Duke University, "When prayer uplifts or calms, it inhibits cortisol, epinephrine, and norepinephrine - hormones that flow out of the adrenal glands in response to stress. These fight-or-flight chemicals, released over time, can compromise the immune system, upping the odds of developing any number of illnesses, including heart disease, stroke, peptic ulcers, and inflammatory bowel disorder (IBS)." See NOTES.

THIRTY MEDICAL SCHOOLS IN AMERICA OFFER COURSES IN FAITH AND MEDICINE

Many doctors believe that if they prayed with their patients before and after surgery or before administering a course of powerful drugs, this treatment might assist in the patient's recovery. Thirty medical schools in America are now offering courses in faith and medicine.

PRAYER REALLY WORKS

"Prayer works," says Dr. Matthews, associate professor of medicine at Georgetown University School of Medicine in Washington, D.C., and senior research fellow at the National Institute for Healthcare Research in Rockville, Maryland. Dr. Matthews has reviewed more than 200 studies linking religious commitment and health, cited in his book, *The Faith Factor*.

Dr. Matthews cites studies suggesting that people who pray are less likely to get sick, are more likely to recover from surgery and illness, and are better able to cope with their illnesses than people who don't pray. Some evidence indicates that sick people who are prayed for also fare significantly better than those who aren't. In fact, some physicians report that people who are prayed for often do better even if they don't know they're being prayed for. See NOTES.

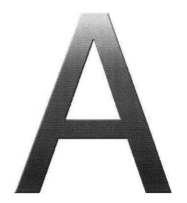

A

Ask, and it shall
be given you; seek,
and ye shall find ...
(Matthew 7:7)

MOSES AND PRAYER

Moses prayed that The Lord's glory would appear unto his children and that God's favour may rest on them. Moses also prayed for the work of our hands to be established by the Lord, because without HIM our work amounts to nothing.

> *Let thy work appear unto thy servants, and thy glory unto their children... And let the beauty of the LORD our God be upon us: and establish thou the work of our hands upon us; yea, the work of our hands establish thou it.* (Psalm 90:16-17)

Later on, Moses tells us that God fulfilled all the promises he made to his people,

> *And, behold, this day I am going the way of all the earth: and ye know in all your hearts and in all your souls, that not one thing hath failed of all the good things which the Lord your God spake concerning you; all are come to pass unto you, and not one thing hath failed thereof.* (Joshua 23:14)

JESUS ABOUT PRAYER

Jesus told us to pray as follows,

Our Father which art in Heaven,
Hallowed be Thy Name.
Thy kingdom come,
Thy will be done
In earth as it is in heaven

Give us this day our daily bread and
Forgive us our debt as we forgive others
And lead us not into temptation
But deliver us from evil
For Thine is the kingdom
And the power and the glory
Forever
Amen.
(Matthew 6:9-15)

This tells us to praise, have faith, and trust. This prayer tells us that God is in charge, we should pray for what we need today, ask for forgiveness, and forgive others. Ask not to be tempted and to be delivered from evil. Acknowledge that God is the ruler of heaven and earth.

In addition, Jesus tells us to have faith, always pray, and never faint (Luke 18:1-8) and that GOD always hears us (John 11:42). That has been my experience too. Try it out and I can near enough guarantee that you'll be very pleasantly surprised!

PRAYER WORKS!

MANY THANKS

Many thanks to all the people who've helped me along the way, and this includes all health professionals and doctors I have consulted over the years. Each and every one helped me along on my path, and many gave me little pieces of information that were useful one way or another and helped me improve my health. Some doctors were instrumental in helping me understand that the medical profession does not always have the answers for all ailments or people.

I learned much and am extremely grateful to the people who have helped me get back on my feet. There are more elaborate credits in my eBook, _My Story of Survival._ (See NOTES.)

I have a special place in my heart for Self-Publishing School and my classmates and buddies. Thank you for your tremendous support and encouragement. (See NOTES.)

I love and embrace the family members and friends who were there for me. This has been on occasion my siblings and various good old friends and neighbours, and particularly my children.

Without my children I would not be able to do this. Thank you to my youngest for your ongoing and unwavering support in all ways. Thank you to my oldest for your tech and graphic design know-how and back up, and for the continuous motivation you provide me to keep going.

I credit my Creator for my good health and for every single breath I take.

INTRO

I honestly cannot remember how many doctors I've seen over the last 15 years. I used to be so healthy. I was married to a doctor and ran 3 medical clinics for a number of years. In addition, I took care of hubby, the kids, our house, and the kids' education.

Eventually I crashed. I crashed so badly that the only place left for me, according to the medical industry, was the too-hard basket.

I've been treated by numerous GPs and medical specialists of all sorts, as well as chiropractors, osteopaths, acupuncturists, homeopaths, massage therapists, and naturopaths. Well, you get the idea, just about anyone in the healing industry. And despite this I went from a healthy and vibrant hardworking mum and wife to a hardly existing human being, only capable of lying in bed and waiting for the end.

After burning out, my health went from bad to worse, from heatstroke to dehydration and pneumonia, heart faltering, pancreatic and gallbladder attacks, intolerance to antibiotics, chemical sensitivities and major allergies, ruptured appendix, septicaemia and orthostatic intolerance. My life had literally become hell to the point where premature death, at times, seemed a desirable option.

In the process, I also lost my job, my relationship, my home, my income, and status in life.

Two smiley faces in the morning is what kept me going, two smiley faces and God's Word.

"Mummy, are you going to die?"

"Oh darling, the Bible tells me that the spirit of God made me and that his breath gave me life. Would He desert his own offspring?

Father, I thank you for blessing my children with a healthy and capable Mum and I pray that in all your will be done.

There now, see, you don't have to worry about anything anymore, our lives are in God's hand and I can think of no better place."

Prior to reading the Bible I worried so much, because as far as I understood it, everything was up to me. I had to take care of whatever needed to be taken care of; all the little worries as well as all the big concerns in life.

But then, as I couldn't sleep at night and tossed and turned, during my darkest hours I found GOD's Word and HIS SON. I fell in love all over again, my spirit lifted, and my health improved.

What I discovered was that healing takes place on numerous levels, and the word 'healthy' means different things to different people.

At the time I thought that I would be healthy if only I were to get up and running again. Little did I realise that the mad rush I called life had very little to do with living, and my routine closely resembled some mad(wo)man racing blindly on a road to nowhere.

Falling head over heels, and this time forever after, didn't only cure some of my ailments; it cured my entire life! My life and spirit are now in God's hands and all is in good order.

All the promises in the Bible are true and there is nothing I'd like to do more than share some of these promises with you and tell you how these have been fulfilled in my life. Speak them out and they will come true for you too!

The following Scripture verses didn't only get me through many sleepless nights and despairing moments, but they literally turned my life around.

GOD'S PROMISES COME TRUE

THE SPIRIT OF GOD HATH MADE ME, AND THE BREATH OF THE ALMIGHTY HATH GIVEN ME *life*.

JOB 33:4

VERSE 1 - THE SPIRIT OF GOD HATH MADE ME AND THE BREATH OF THE ALMIGHTY HATH GIVEN ME LIFE.

GOD's spirit made me, and it is His breath that gave me life. Say no more.

What better place was there for me to turn to, when I found myself in a tight spot and wasn't able to find help, no matter where I looked?

I worked in the medical industry as a practice manager; my husband was a 'holistic health practitioner' who besides conventional medicine also practised homeopathy, Chinese herbs, acupuncture, and anthroposophical medicine. If those treatments wouldn't heal me, then what would?

The Bible mentions a lady with a medical issue who suffered greatly under the care of many doctors for twelve years. She spent everything she had, and instead of getting better she got worse (Mark 5:2-34, Luke 8:43-48). She then turned to Jesus and was healed instantaneously.

I had old family friends pulling out all stops to arrange yet another batch of tests for me.

"We'll run a few more tests to see what the issue is and why you cannot return to business as usual."

"But Doctor Danny, last year we did similar tests and nothing of any great significance showed up that would explain why any of this is happening to me."

"Don't worry, this time around you'll only be out of pocket for around $450. The rest will be covered by Medicare."

I found myself in a spot similar to the Biblical lady with the medical issue, where for well over a decade I actually spent much *more* than I had and only got sicker and sicker. That was until I found GOD's Word and started to apply His truth and wisdom to my life.

If God's spirit made me, and His breath gave me life, this makes me His child, and as such I should I go to Him and His Son for help.

Jesus said,

> *"Do not call anyone on earth 'father,' for you have one Father, and he is in heaven."* (Matthew 23:9)

That is the Father I turned to and asked for advice.

"Father, shall I commit to one more test?"

I heard loud and clear, *"My child, you should rest."*

GOD IS LIFE

O LORD MY GOD,

I CRIED UNTO THEE, AND THOU HAST *healed* ME.

PSALM 30:2

VERSE 2 - O LORD MY GOD I CRIED UNTO THEE AND THOU HAST HEALED ME.

To say that I cried to GOD is way beyond an understatement. I pleaded and bargained, I wept and sobbed, I shed many tears. I literally begged for my life.

When I suffered a severe pancreatic attack my GP was quite desperate to get me into the hospital. But by then I had come to rely on the Lord and it was Him I turned to. My GP visited me twice a day urging me to allow him to phone an ambulance to get me into the hospital.

"Mimi, when you die, I'll be in trouble, they'll investigate me because you belong in the hospital right now."

"Dr. Kean, I'll take full responsibility and will sign whatever you would like me to sign to absolve you from this responsibility. But I 'have done' hospitals and tests and diagnoses for ten years and this got me nowhere. I'll be praying from now on."

I am not in any way saying that people should not seek medical attention when their doctors suggest this. I always recommend that everyone follow his or her doctor's advice.

But for me at that time, in the year 2008, I had followed doctors' advice for as much as possible for at least a decade and not achieved positive results. I happened to have one of those 'burnout' conditions where the immune system had gone AWOL, and whatever I attempted in the way of tests and treatment seemed to deplete my energy even more.

I said, *"Lord, what should I do, what do you suggest?"* And the answer came back, *"Mimi, just rest!"*

It took a ruptured appendix and septicaemia before I truly heeded that advice, because by then I really did not have any other choice.

I was laid up in bed for years. There is a wonderful gospel song by Pat Lewis from the 103rd Street Gospel Choir, and she sings, "I know that God hears prayer... I could have been dead a long time ago... laid up in bed... down to my last dime... no help at all... God heard her call." God heard Pat Lewis' call and he heard mine too. (See NOTES.)

I begged, I pleaded, I cried, and I received way more than my life, I received peace and joy and comfort and love, hope and a future. I received healing way beyond what I expected because I didn't even realise at the time how much my whole life and mind and spirit needed healing.

GOD's Word heals all wounds and all ails. If you feel like you're at the end of the road, why don't you give it a whirl? Say, *'LORD, Mimi told me that you got her out of a tight spot, I can do with a little help too.'* I know that The LORD will hear you because that is the promise in His Holy WORD.

I cried to God and He healed me.

GOD HEARS PRAYER

THE **LORD** PRESERVETH THE *simple*: I WAS BROUGHT LOW, AND **HE** HELPED ME.

PSALM 116:6

VERSE 3 - THE LORD PRESERVETH THE SIMPLE: I WAS BROUGHT LOW, AND HE HELPED ME.

If you think that you need to be some kind of a bigwig to get help or have a whole congregation praying for you to be heard, you're thinking wrong. GOD loves simple people.

In the year 1999 it was not only my health that crashed, but also my relationship. My job disappeared, and my children and I were homeless for around a year.

I told my children how exciting it was for us to be on this holiday, and at ages 11 and 13 they bought this.

We drove around Australia with a trailer that was just big enough to hold our bedding. We did this for a year. I was brought very low. I cried out to The LORD and He heard me.

I'm in good company. The Bible is filled with stories where people cry out to GOD and he hears them. For instance, Hannah, the wife of Elkanah, was granted her wish for children, and the same for Leah, Jacob's wife. Also, a certain woman of the wives of the prophets not only kept her sons, but in addition was blessed to the extent that she was able to pay off her debts (1 Samuel 1 and 2, Genesis 29 and 30, 2 Kings 4).

I was very simple and very low and GOD helped me.

THE LORD HEARD AND HELPED ME

GOD CREATED MAN IN *HIS* OWN IMAGE, IN THE IMAGE OF *GOD* CREATED *HE* THEM.. MALE AND FEMALE CREATED *HE* THEM.

GENESIS 1:27

VERSE 4 - GOD CREATED MAN IN HIS OWN IMAGE, IN THE IMAGE OF GOD CREATED HE THEM... MALE AND FEMALE CREATED HE THEM.

Once I realised that we are created in GOD's image I knew that not even the sky is the limit. Often enough it is our own thinking that limits us. The knowledge that GOD made me in His own image means that potentially, if I were to live up to it, I would be capable of much and able to contribute in ways I had never even thought were possible.

One thing is for sure, with that kind of blueprint, there is no reason for me to be lying about for years on end, licking my wounds.

Reading those verses was a massive incentive for me to recognise that, *'Hey there is more to me than I thought there was, and I better start living up to my potential, or otherwise I'm merely taking up air and space, and that's no example to set for my children.'*

If I was made in God's image, I should start living like one of His children. What did this mean for me?

I realised that God created the world by the breath of His mouth. This is how he created life.

> *In the beginning God created the heaven and the earth...*
> *By the word of the Lord the heavens were made, their starry host by the breath of his mouth.*
>
> *And the Lord God formed man of the dust of the ground, and breathed into his nostrils the breath of life; and man became a living soul.* (Genesis 1:1, Psalm 33:6, Genesis 2:7)

God's Word is life and creates life. I decided that my words should do the same. And so no more negative talk of any kind. The best kind of words to me are the uplifting, life-giving words of Scripture.

And that's why I am sharing these with you on my websites www.mosaichouse.co and here in my book *God Healed Me*.

I want to share that God's Word heals and brings life because it did for me.

MADE IN GOD'S IMAGE

THOU HAST DELIVERED **MY SOUL** FROM **DEATH**, AND MINE EYES FROM **TEARS**...

PSALM 116:8

VERSE 5 - THOU HAST DELIVERED MY SOUL FROM DEATH, AND MINE EYES FROM TEARS.

I've literally been pulled back from the brink of death so many times that I cannot count the number.

I've been in a number of car crashes where the car was written off. My children and I survived an occasion where my out-of-control car was sliding on oil down a hill heading toward a ravine, whilst on another occasion our car jumped off the gravel into a copse of trees.

I survived two nasty cases of double pneumonia, heart faltering, and pancreatic attacks, as well as a ruptured appendix with septicaemia whilst intolerant to antibiotics.

The surgeon refused to operate because he was convinced that the odds were greatly stacked against me. Hence I still have my appendix. There's plenty more, but it will suffice to say that I've been close to death many times, and my heavenly Father saved me each and every time and wiped my tears, and even put a smile on my face and kept my spirits up throughout all the challenges.

How did a Scripture verse like this help when I was in trouble?

> *Thou hast delivered my soul from death and mine eyes from tears.* (Psalm 116:8)

About a year after I ruptured my appendix my daughters finally managed to get a doctor to come out and see me at home. (More about this in *My Story of Survival*.)

When doctors had pretty much given up on me having a life or any quality of life, I read this Scripture verse and thought, *"God is with me, I am still alive against the odds, I am not even crying because I am so confident that I'll pull through because God is with me."*

"Mum, the doctor is here to check up on you."

After a thorough investigation this friendly GP gave me his verdict.

"The main thing, Mimi, is to get you comfortable and make it all manageable for you."

I looked at the doctor as he was packing his medical case to continue on his home visits. Comfortable and manageable? Hell, no!

I am going to get better, if the Lord will!
I smiled at him.

"Thank you, Doctor Dylan." I was seething.

The words 'comfortable' and 'manageable' are dirty words to me. For someone in my situation, a woman in the prime of her life, with two teenage daughters to take care of, these are words of despair and words that tell me that there is no hope for me and I'll never get better.

I utterly and completely reject the words 'comfortable' and 'manageable' in the context they were spoken to me.

So what if I'm not back to where I used to be, and still looking and feeling rather frail?

Sometimes physical reality does not match the truth of the matter... yet.

Tomorrow is another day filled with new hope and encouragement from the Holy Word.

I will heal thee. (2 Kings 20:5)

All anxiety and hopelessness simply vanishes into nothingness when I open my Bible and read these encouraging words: words of hope and comfort and love and healing. Those words are truth. What is happening in my life right now is simply playing catch-up.

I know that God's Word brings light where there is darkness, and we all know that darkness cannot exist where there is light.

Negative words and conditions are darkness. God's Word is light: Speak light!

Your word is a lamp for my feet, a light on my path.
(Psalm 119:105)

SAVED FROM DEATH

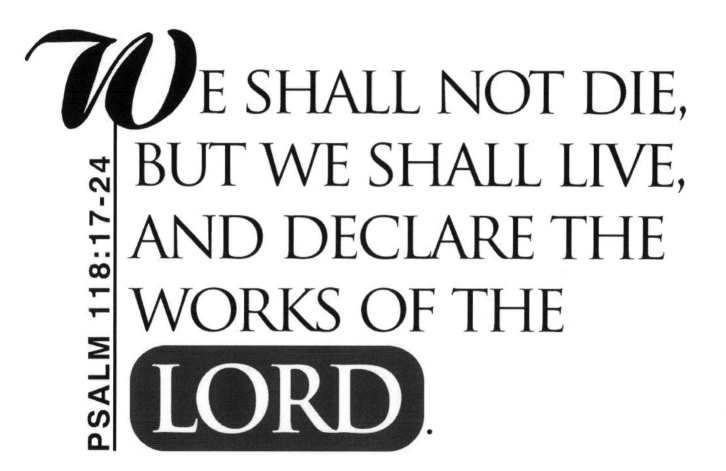

WE SHALL NOT DIE, BUT WE SHALL LIVE, AND DECLARE THE WORKS OF THE LORD.

PSALM 118:17-24

VERSE 6 - WE SHALL NOT DIE, BUT WE SHALL LIVE, AND DECLARE THE WORKS OF THE LORD.

I had no idea that there were these kinds of promises in the Bible.

> *I shall not die but I shall live and declare the works of the LORD.* (Psalm 118:17-24)

I say "Amen" to that.

There's more to this verse than meets the eye. "I shall not die" for me so far has meant that I'm still around to tell my tale, and there is nothing I like better than sharing Scripture verses and sharing how these verses have impacted my life in such a positive way. I like nothing better than telling my story because in my life, it is my faith and these verses that pulled me through and kept me in the land of the living.

But the promise here is also that I may not die the second death, and that sounds pretty awesome to me! If you haven't heard of the second death before, open the book of Revelation and/or read our book on living forever.

I had so much time to think about what I wanted to do, if I wouldn't die.

I simply thought, *"What do I enjoy doing most?"*

The answer is quite self-evident.

"It is reading and sharing Scripture."

I DECLARE THE WORKS OF THE LORD

O GIVE THANKS UNTO THE (LORD); THOSE PLANTED IN *HIS* HOUSE SHALL *flourish* IN *HIS* COURTS, THEY SHALL BRING FORTH *fruit* IN OLD AGE.

PSALMS 118:29, 92:13-15

Verse 7 - O give thanks unto the LORD; those planted in his house shall flourish in his courts, they shall bring forth fruit in old age.

Hahaha, Thank you Father!

Those planted in his house shall flourish and bring forth fruit in old age.

I like to think that the LORD may restore to me the years that the locust hath eaten (Joel 2:25).

If The Lord will, I'll keep going and going and be semi-retired forever after whilst sharing Scripture verses around. It is GOD's Word, which helps me so much in my life. Applying GOD's Word has restored everything that had gone kaput, way over and beyond my wildest dreams and expectations.

So far, I've opened a gift shop and designed a Free Scripture Card website. I've written a book called *My Story of Survival* and another one called *Mimi's Book Launch Plan*.

Most people at my age are starting to slow down; I'm only just beginning... I'm stoked!

I was reading this verse more than a decade ago when I started to read the Bible in earnest. I believed it. I saw no physical evidence for it, but believed it and held onto it and prayed for it to become true in my life and trusted that it would.

I thanked the Lord for His kindness towards my children and myself. I praised the Lord for making this come true in my life.

I realised that what we call 'facts' do not always represent 'the truth.' And I waited patiently for The Lord to have the truth manifest in my life.

BRING FORTH FRUIT IN OLD AGE

VERSE 8 - I WILL WALK BEFORE THE LORD IN THE LAND OF THE LIVING.

More than once did my doctor tell me that I was the sickest patient in his clinic. He gently tried to prepare me for the worst and urged me to organise for this.

"Mimi, you need to know that there is no one in my practice as crook (Aussie slang for sick/unwell) as you are."

"I know, I know… so what."

I knew what he was talking about but I refused to be part of his reality. I also knew that GOD hears prayers, not because I deserve to be heard or earned this or anything like that, but simply because our GOD is a merciful GOD. I decided to walk with GOD and His Word.

One day I opened my Bible and there it was, the words:

'I will walk before the LORD in the land of the living.'

Those were the words I held onto. I shook off the words of all others and I stopped visiting the well-meaning doctors with ready tests and sticky labels of all kinds of diagnoses of ailments.

Instead I curled up in bed, revised my diet, and I prayed. My children prayed. And we relied on the words,

'I will walk before the LORD in the land of the living.'

And that is exactly what I am doing now! Walking and living before the LORD. Another promise fulfilled in my life!

WALK BEFORE THE LORD
IN THE LAND OF THE LIVING

LORD, WE ARE NOT WORTHY… BUT SPEAK THE **WORD** ONLY, AND WE SHALL BE *healed*.

MATTHEW 8:8

VERSE 9 - LORD, WE ARE NOT WORTHY... BUT SPEAK THE WORD ONLY AND WE SHALL BE HEALED.

Did I feel worthy to be healed? Hell, no. I mucked up, big time! I never rested, rarely ate, barely slept, I never for a moment regarded any potential limitations a body may have. And obviously there is a price to pay for that.

Okay, so I did this in my ignorance and eagerness to perform well... there is still a price to be paid for ignoring human limitations and acting like some super human who does not need sleep or sustenance and so on. The last thing I expected was for someone to bail me out.

Eventually curling up in a ball and waiting for the end was about the extent of my expectations... until I picked up the Bible and read,

> *Lord, we are not worthy... but speak the word only, and we shall be healed.* (Matthew 8:8)

Would I be so bold and dare ask for a favour? For the sake of my children, yes I did.

I said,

> '*Lord, I am not worthy... but speak the word only, and I shall be healed.*'

How amazingly life-changing it was for me to believe in and hold onto that promise.

For five years I lived on a ten-ingredient-only diet for breakfast, lunch, and dinner. This diet, which contained oodles of faith, combined with the resting, helped me slowly regain my strength.

Nowadays I eat more than ten ingredients, and every week I manage to incorporate more items into my diet.

WE SHALL BE HEALED

*A*s THOU HAST *believed*, SO BE IT DONE UNTO THEE. AND **HIS** SERVANT WAS *healed* IN THE SELFSAME HOUR.

MATTHEW 8:13

VERSE 10 - AS THOU HAST BELIEVED, SO BE IT DONE UNTO THEE. AND HIS SERVANT WAS HEALED IN THE SELFSAME HOUR.

I didn't just read the promises in the Bible and I didn't only say them out loud and share them with my family. I believed the promises to be true, then and now, with all my heart and all my soul; they are like reality to me.

Believe and you shall receive. (Mark 11:24)

My daughter had a premonition that came true. She saw and heard a doctor tell her that my chances of survival weren't great. She came to me in tears to share her premonition with me. I did not hesitate for a second, but responded that our lives are in God's hands, and whatever God's will for our life is, is fine by me.

Her premonition came with a warning for me not to accept pain relief, and we didn't. Obedience to this warning may be what saved my life.

As thou has believed so be it done unto thee. (Matthew 8:13)

I believe that God has my best interest at heart, and I know this to be true because many good promises have been fulfilled in my life and all through history. Since the beginning of time, GOD's promises and the fulfilment of them have played themselves out and been faithfully recorded in the Bible. They've been recorded in the history book of the Jewish nation.

Thank you, Jewish people, for keeping this testimony safe and passing these witness accounts on to us.

Are these promises only for Jewish people or only for Christian people? No, these promises are for anyone that loves GOD's Word and follows his directions.

'For mine house shall be called a house of prayer for all people.' Whosoever will. (Isaiah 56:7, Revelations 22:17)

AS YOU BELIEVE SHALL YOU RECEIVE

HIMSELF TOOK OUR *infirmities,* AND BARE OUR *sicknesses.*

MATTHEW 8:17

VERSE 11 - HIMSELF TOOK OUR INFIRMITIES, AND BARE OUR SICKNESSES.

Jesus died so that we may live.

> *He gave His only begotten Son, that whosoever believeth in Him should not perish, but have everlasting life.'* (1 John 4:9, John 3:16)

Jesus is the living word and the perfect role model who showed what is expected from those who claim to love GOD and His Word (John 1:14, 1 John 3:5).

JESUS EXPOSED EVIL AND HYPOCRISY

Jesus' sinless life exposed the evil and hypocrisy of those around him. His perfect conduct sharply contrasted the pretence of his contemporaries. This got so up the nose of the religious folk of his time that all the clergy could think of was to eliminate Jesus, to prevent people from finding them out for the phonies that they were. They crucified HIM who showed us the right way (John 3:16-21, 15:22).

Jesus went out of his way to heal anyone who was in need of healing, and after this he allowed himself to be brought as a lamb to the slaughter and be crucified, not for his own sins but for the sins of this world.

> *Many good works have I shewed you from my Father; for which of those works do ye stone me?* (John 10:32, 18:37)

Jesus set us an example to live up to. It's simple and straightforward. Be good and do good and don't be surprised if you get punished for your good deeds.

Use the talents you were given to help wherever you are. It's never between them and you, it's always between you and God.

Give the world the best you have,
and it may never be enough.
Give the best you've got anyway.

In the final analysis it is between you and God;
it was never between you and them anyway.
Mother Theresa

HE BARE OUR SICKNESSES

FEAR THOU NOT;
FOR **I AM** WITH THEE:
BE NOT DISMAYED;
FOR I AM THY GOD:
I WILL STRENGTHEN
THEE; YEA, I WILL
HELP THEE; YEA,
I WILL *uphold* THEE...

ISAIAH 41:10

VERSE 12 - FEAR THOU NOT; FOR I AM WITH THEE: BE NOT DISMAYED; FOR I AM THY GOD: I WILL STRENGTHEN THEE; YEA, I WILL HELP THEE; YEA, I WILL UPHOLD THEE...

Where did I look for comfort when I was so ill, on my own and couldn't sleep at night? I used to turn on the TV, but eventually, the swearing, the sex, the violence, the bad news streaming into my bedroom every night, I couldn't hack it and I turned to GOD's WORD.

Initially, I looked for His Word on the TV and started watching religious programs, but soon I couldn't handle the interpretations given to GOD's WORD by overzealous preachers who seemed keener to fill their own coffers than to share Scripture as it is written.

I managed to get hold of a laptop and installed the software program e-Sword, which helped me find Scripture verses that applied to my situation. I desperately needed someone to tell me that everything was going to be all right.

Every night when I laid down to sleep, I felt as if I was going to die. I had this tremendous cloud of doom hanging over my entire bedroom, and no matter what childhood rhymes I sang to myself, or what positive thinking I applied, I could not find calm or peace. For years I went to sleep thinking that I would not wake up in the morning. Then one day, I found that it is written,

> *Fear thou not; for I am with thee: be not dismayed; for I am thy God: I will strengthen thee; yea, I will help thee; yea, I will uphold thee with the right hand of my righteousness.* (Isaiah 41:10)

I read this verse and I cannot begin to tell you how much comfort this gave me. I tried to remember this verse at night to comfort myself, but with anxiety and despair swirling through my brain and heart I wasn't able to remember the words.

I highlighted these comforting words in my Bible and still could not find them at night because I have so many highlighted words in my Bible. I bookmarked the words... but I had so many bookmarks throughout my Bible.

Eventually I cut A4 sheets of paper in large squares and wrote the Scripture verses on these bits of paper. I put melodies to the Scripture verses and sang them to myself at night and to my children in the morning. This is what got me through.

It literally took me weeks, if not months, to organise these square bits of paper with Scripture verses on them. I organised a little stack of these Scripture verses on my bedside table right next to me. So that whenever I needed comfort at any time in the night, I had the appropriate text at my fingertips, Once I was able to recall these words, they chased out the doom and gloom in no time.

God's Word truly is life and brings calm and comfort,

> *Fear thou not; for I am with thee: be not dismayed; for I am thy God: I will strengthen thee; yea, I will help thee; yea, I will uphold thee...*

Slowly, slowly I started to get more sleep because many of my demons were chased away by the Holy Word. And so, with God's help, I became a little stronger.

Oh joy, another promise fulfilled.

I WILL STRENGHTEN THEE

THEY BROUGHT UNTO **HIM** MANY THAT WERE POSSESSED WITH *DEVILS*... **HE** CAST OUT THE *SPIRITS* WITH **HIS** WORD, AND *healed* ALL THAT WERE SICK.

MATTHEW 8:16

Verse 13 - They brought unto him many that were possessed with devils... he cast out the spirits with his word, and healed ALL that were sick.

I have seen many doctors and healers over the years and they all had a few things in common. For instance, all of them healed *some* patients but not *all*.

And all of the healers and doctors I consulted had some area of expertise. In my travels I have never come across a doctor or healer who knows everything there is to know about healing, nor have I met someone who healed every single patient they treated. Doctors and healers are only human, after all.

My hero Jesus, on the other hand, healed everyone: people with foul spirits, as well as all other kind of diseases.

Unbeknownst to me I was filled with foul spirits. I was filled to the brim with spirits of fear, despair, hopelessness, inadequacy, despondency, failure, rejection, and guess what? Jesus rebuked them all, cast them out, and off they went!

How did Jesus cast them out?

> *But if I with the finger of God cast out devils, no doubt the kingdom of God is come upon you.*
>
> *He said, It is written, Man shall not live by bread alone, but by every word that proceedeth out of the mouth of God.* (Matthew 4:4, Luke 11:20)

That's right, my friends, He cast out devils with His Word. He chased the demons and foul spirits out with the Holy Word.

First, I did not recognise that I had such bad spirits in me. I always tried to do the right thing by everyone... it was other people, right?

Wrong! It was me that was filled to the brim with hopelessness.

Sure, superficially I said and did all the right things, but my heart was fearful and my spirit was low, very low.

Instead of relying on the Lord and speaking His Truth into my life, I had allowed my demons to get the better of me.

But no more. Once I started to read the Bible daily and experience the life and power in the Holy Word, there was no stopping me.

"You're useless now and rejected, you may as well die," is what my demons told me.

I fought this with, *"You liar, I'm a child of God who has plans for my success and a good future."* (1 John 3:1, Jeremiah 29:11)

"You'll never ever get better, all that any of your doctors hope for is to 'manage' your condition and that is best-case scenario."

"You liar, God says, "I am the Lord that healeth thee," and I believe Him over you any day!" (Exodus 15:26)

Remember, how earlier I mentioned that it may take it little while for the truth to manifest in your life? Sure Jesus cast out spirits and off they went. But for little ol' me, it may take a little longer.

But out they go. No more idle words, just God's Holy Word to cast out my demons.

> *Every idle word that men shall speak, they shall give account thereof in the day of judgment. For by thy words thou shalt be justified, and by thy words thou shalt be condemned.* (Matthew 12:36-37)

We're supposed to love each other as we love ourselves. It is time to apply this wisdom to myself.

CAST OUT SPIRITS

...*I* AM THE LORD THAT *healeth* THEE.

EXODUS 15:26

Verse 14 - I am the Lord that healeth thee.

Where do we go for our healing? I used to turn to doctors and natural healers; that was before I discovered GOD's Word. Nowadays my faith is in the LORD.

Don't doctors and other medical and natural practitioners heal? Sure they do... sometimes, but not at other times, and occasionally some of them get it wrong altogether.

A friend of mine was diagnosed with a terminal illness and tried every treatment possible; orthodox as well as alternative. She died a few months after she had been 'given a few months to live' by her doctors. Weeks before her death, she cried out to me and said, *'I should have gone to God, I should have turned to Him.'*

Does that mean that my friend would have stayed alive had she turned to God? No one has the answer to that. But chances are that she may have had more peace in her heart and found a way of dealing with her situation if she had put her faith in God. By her own admission, she didn't do that and experienced pure agony and despair when all the medical diagnoses and treatments didn't bring healing.

It is good to remember that healing takes place on many different levels and physical healing is only a small part of the larger picture.

I advise anyone to go and see his or her health practitioner for advice with any kind of ailment and follow the advice given if this seems appropriate.

However, if this fails, again and again, then maybe you would like to fall onto your knees and lift your eyes and see what happens. It worked for me, and now is my first choice and not my last. And it works better for me than any remedy I've ever been prescribed.

Scripture tells us that,

> *'If thou wilt diligently hearken to the voice of the Lord thy God, and wilt do that which is right in his sight, and wilt give ear to his commandments, and keep all his statutes, I will put none of these diseases upon thee, which I have brought upon the Egyptians: for I am the Lord that healeth thee.'*

Remember how I mentioned earlier that there is a success formula with at least 3 points to keep in mind for successful prayer?

Here are some additional points if you're praying for healing,
1. Listen to what God tells you.
2. Do what is right according to Him.
3. Follow His commandments and rules.

In addition, Jesus told his disciples on one occasion when they failed to heal a sick child, this was:

Because of your unbelief: for verily I say unto you, If ye have faith as a grain of mustard seed, ye shall say unto this mountain, Remove hence to yonder place; and it shall remove; and nothing shall be impossible unto you.

Howbeit this kind goeth not out but by prayer and fasting. (Mark 17:15-21)

Due to various medical conditions I cannot fast on food but I have fasted on words many times. Keep this in mind when there are obstacles that won't budge. Jesus recommended a combination of prayer and fasting on this particular occasion.

THE LORD HEALS

THOU SHALT BE *blessed* ABOVE ALL PEOPLE.... THE LORD WILL TAKE AWAY FROM THEE ALL SICKNESS.

DEUTERONOMY 7:14-15

VERSE 15 - THOU SHALT BE BLESSED ABOVE ALL PEOPLE... THE LORD WILL TAKE AWAY FROM THEE ALL SICKNESS.

The Bible is filled with promises. We're told that the people who choose to follow GOD's directions and commandments have been chosen *'to be a special people.'* (Deuteronomy 7) These directions we are to follow are also called moral guidelines or the golden rule, summed up by Jesus as, *"Do unto others"* (Exodus 20, Deuteronomy 5, Leviticus 19:18, 34, Luke 6:31, Matthew 7:12).

I know, I know, there are people who can drink, eat, smoke, and seemingly do whatever they want, appearing to be in good health without adverse consequences. This is what God's Word has to say about some of them,

If they hear not Moses and the prophets, neither will they be persuaded, though one rose from the dead. (Luke 16:31)

The promise is that if we do as we are told, we shall be blessed and the LORD will take away all sickness.

Without a doubt there appear to be exceptions where, for reasons we don't always understand, very good and sincere people suffer much.

As far as I'm concerned, it always pays to check and see if we're doing all the right things before we assume that we perhaps could be one of these exceptions.

THE LORD WILL TAKE AWAY ALL SICKNESS

JESUS SAID, O *WOMAN*, GREAT IS THY *faith*: BE IT UNTO THEE EVEN AS THOU WILT. HER DAUGHTER WAS *MADE WHOLE* FROM THAT VERY HOUR.

MATTHEW 15:28

VERSE 16 - JESUS SAID, O WOMAN, GREAT IS THY FAITH: BE IT UNTO THEE EVEN AS THOU WILT. HER DAUGHTER WAS MADE WHOLE FROM THAT VERY HOUR.

I mentioned in the previous chapter that people who follow GOD's directions are blessed. Scripture also tells us stories about people who weren't of the Jewish faith or heritage and who were not following Jesus either. Yet their faith healed them.

This particular woman begged Jesus three times to please heal her daughter who was *'grievously vexed with a devil.'* (Matthew 15:22)

Despite the disciples wanting to send this woman of Canaan away, and despite Jesus initially ignoring her, this lady continued to plead and beg for her daughter to be cured.

Eventually Jesus relented and said,

> *'O woman, great is thy faith: be it unto thee even as thou wilt. Her daughter was made whole from that very hour.'* (Matthew 15:22-28)

What does that tell me? It tells me to never judge others (religious or not), to never give up asking for healing either for others or myself. It tells me to be patient. And this account from the Bible tells me to have faith.

Don't allow others to dictate what you can and cannot ask for.

BE IT UNTO THEE EVEN AS THOU WILT

THE *PRAYER OF FAITH* SHALL SAVE THE SICK, AND THE LORD SHALL *raise* HIM UP.

JAMES 5:15

Verse 17 - The prayer of faith shall save the sick, and the Lord shall raise him up.

James, an elder in the church, tells us that 'the prayer of faith shall save the sick and the LORD shall raise him up; and if he has committed sins, they shall be forgiven him.'

When I found myself at death's door, this literally meant that there was nothing to lose and only to gain. After having consulted so many different doctors without a cure or relief in sight, but instead coming away with all kinds of undesirable sticky labels plastered all over me, what was left for me was to either give up and crawl into a hole or look up to heaven and say, *"Help me, please."* Lame-ass... I know, but true.

I am so happy that I put my faith in GOD's Word and not in man's word. In *My Story of Survival* I recall a situation in the hospital where I prayed for The Lord to raise me up and as the team of physicians walked in, I was literally touching the ceiling! (See NOTES.)

As far as I am concerned, God has a terrific sense of humour!

RAISE ME UP PLEASE!

PRAY ONE FOR ANOTHER, THAT YE MAY BE *healed*. THE FERVENT *prayer* OF A *RIGHTEOUS MAN* AVAILETH MUCH.

JAMES 5:16

VERSE 18 - PRAY ONE FOR ANOTHER, THAT YE MAY BE HEALED. THE FERVENT PRAYER OF A RIGHTEOUS MAN AVAILETH MUCH.

At times it was just my girls praying for me. There were also occurrences where others and I myself joined in.

Recently I had a friend pray for me regarding a persisting problem in my life regarding the life situation of a loved one. Within one week the situation changed dramatically for the better.

One day after our conversation there was an interview, the next day a job offer, the next day signing of contract, the next day offer of accommodation, the next day signing of lease.' This happened after more than a year and a half of unemployment and continuous moving around.

When I finally confided in a friend and she prayed for me and my loved one, the situation turned around for good in *one week*, miraculous!

The Bible tells us that,

> *'The fervent prayer of a righteous man availeth much.'*

The prayer of the prophet Elijah is referred to in this Scripture verse and how he was a human being just like us, and he,

> *'Prayed earnestly that it might not rain: and it rained not on the earth by the space of three years and six months.'*

Prayer has proven to be the most powerful medicine for our family and has never failed us. It is instantly accessible, and for us the most effective and comforting remedy.

SURVEY ON PRAYER

A survey on prayer from Belief.net (see NOTES) shows us that 68% of Christians pray more than once a day. More than 70% of all Christians and Jewish people pray for health and safety, and respectively 93% and 74% pray for God's guidance.

Only 0.6% of Christians think that their prayers are never answered whilst 2.9% of Jewish people think the same.

In contrast a whopping 43% of Christians say that their prayers are often answered whilst 27.5% says that they are ALWAYS answered.

This is in contrast to Jewish people who say that 12.7% of their prayers are always answered and 33.1% often.

PRAYING FOR FAMILY

More than 50% of Christians and Jewish people pray most often for family.

When asked if, in the past six months people had prayed for them, more than 80% of Christians said yes, friends and family have prayed for them, whilst 56.7% of Jewish people had friends and family pray for them.

Nearly 40% of Christians had people in their religious community pray for them, whilst this was just over 20% for Jewish people who had people in their community pray for them.

'Prayer warriors' and others prayed for 28% of Christians and 8.1% of Jewish people.

Only 9.2% of Christians said that no one prayed for them in the last 6 months, whilst 35.3% of Jewish people said the same.

75.8% of Christians felt that the prayer helped and 44% of Jewish people felt that when someone prayed for them it helped.

Only 1.9% of Christians did not feel that the prayer had helped and 6.7% of the Jewish faith felt the same.

PRAY FOR ANOTHER

*W*HO DID *SIN*…
THAT HE WAS BORN BLIND?
Jesus SAID, NEITHER HATH
THIS MAN SINNED, NOR HIS
PARENTS: BUT THAT THE
WORKS OF GOD SHOULD
BE MADE MANIFEST IN HIM.

JOHN 9:2-3

VERSE 19 - *WHO DID SIN... THAT HE WAS BORN BLIND?* JESUS SAID, NEITHER HATH THIS MAN SINNED, NOR HIS PARENTS: BUT THAT THE WORKS OF GOD SHOULD BE MADE MANIFEST IN HIM.

Jesus' disciples seemed to assume that the sins of someone in the family had caused this man's blindness. Jesus' response may have come as a surprise to his apostles. He said,

> *Neither hath this man sinned, nor his parents: but that the works of God should be made manifest in him.* (John 9:1-3)

Wow! That's good to hear. People's illnesses are not always caused by their bad actions or decisions.

According to Jesus, the blind man's disability was so that

GOD's work should be made manifest in him.

In Job one and two we read how the devil is allowed to test Job by taking all he has, including the life of his children, his health, and his wealth, and yet, Job does not blame God. It does not appear from reading the Bible that Job did anything at all to bring these calamities upon himself.

I caused a lot of my own troubles, but not necessarily all of them.

Jesus' words are a warning to us all not to point the finger. It is nice to know that sometimes our misfortune may be part of GOD's plan, and all we need to do is stay on that narrow path whilst applying with all our might our mustard-seed-sized faith.

THE WORKS OF GOD BE MADE MANIFEST

HE GIVETH *power* TO THE FAINT; AND TO THEM THAT HAVE NO MIGHT **HE** INCREASETH *strength*... THEY THAT WAIT UPON THE LORD RENEW THEIR STRENGTH...

ISAIAH 40:29-31

VERSE 20 - HE GIVETH POWER TO THE FAINT; AND TO THEM THAT HAVE NO MIGHT HE INCREASETH STRENGTH... THEY THAT WAIT UPON THE LORD SHALL RENEW THEIR STRENGTH...

Here are more promises that if we wait for GOD to save us, he will not fail us. The full verses read,

He giveth power to the faint; and to them that have no might he increaseth strength. Even the youths shall faint and be weary, and the young men shall utterly fall:

But they that wait upon the Lord shall renew their strength; they shall mount up with wings as eagles; they shall run, and not be weary; and they shall walk, and not faint.

My health improved with leaps and bounds only after I stopped consulting doctors and other health professionals. Well-meaning as they may have been, the examinations and tests didn't heal but merely depleted my energy and my bank account.

As soon as I gave up and said, *"LORD it is between You and me only,"* that is when my health started to improve steadily.

HE GIVETH POWER TO THE FAINT

144

HEAL ME, O **LORD**, AND I SHALL BE *healed*; SAVE ME, AND I SHALL BE *saved*: FOR THOU ART *MY PRAISE.*

JEREMIAH 17:14

VERSE 21 - HEAL ME, O LORD, AND I SHALL BE HEALED; SAVE ME, AND I SHALL BE SAVED: FOR THOU ART MY PRAISE.

Thank you, Father, for hearing my prayer, and thank you for healing my family and pouring your blessings out over anyone who reads your promises and has the faith to believe and trust in you.

> *Blessed is the man that trusteth in the Lord, and whose hope the Lord is.* (Jeremiah 17:7)

We prayed that I may be able to get up from my bed and I did. We prayed that I would be walking around again, and albeit tentatively, I am. We're praying that I'll be able to eat whatever I fancy and go for walks and jogs on the beach again and, *if the LORD will*, this also will be a reality in my life.

Praise the LORD!

THOU ART MY PRAISE

*T*HUS SAITH THE **LORD** ... I HAVE HEARD THY *prayer*, I HAVE SEEN THY *tears*: BEHOLD, I WILL *HEAL* THEE:

2 KINGS 20:5

Verse 22 - Thus saith the Lord... I have heard thy prayer, I have seen thy tears: behold, I will heal thee...

When the prophet Isaiah told King Hezekiah that his days on earth were about to come to an end, he wept and prayed to GOD begging for more time. He reminded GOD that he had been a good guy and GOD responded by saying,

> 'I have heard thy prayer, I have seen thy tears: behold, I will heal thee... I will add unto thy days fifteen years.' (2 Kings 20:5, Isaiah 38:5)

Hezekiah was given an extra fifteen years after he had been told that his time was up and he begged for more.

That is another promise for us and another reassurance that indeed GOD hears prayer.

After I read that, there was no stopping me with my prayers. Hezekiah said that he had been a good king. I couldn't claim the same but, *"I have two children and they are just innocent bystanders, maybe some extra time for their sakes... please?"*

Initially, I thought that my time on earth had come to an end, but then I read God's promises and these opened up new horizons. I held on to God's promises with all my might.

> *He healeth the broken in heart, and bindeth up their wounds.* (Psalm 147:3)

I have confidence, knowing that all is in GOD's hands and I have faith as least the size of a tiny seed. (Matthew 17:20, Luke 17:6)

I WILL HEAL THEE

I WILL *restore* HEALTH UNTO THEE, AND I WILL *heal* THEE OF THY WOUNDS, SAITH THE LORD ...

JEREMIAH 30:17

Verse 23 - I will restore health unto thee, and I will heal thee of thy wounds, saith the LORD...

This is what the LORD said to his chosen people, the nation he calls His own. If this is the promise GOD made to a whole nation, how easy for the LORD to heal a family or just one single person?

How powerful these words are to me, the fact that the Creator of Heaven and Earth is concerned enough with a small nation to promise to restore health unto them and heal them of their wounds.

It means the world to me that our Father in Heaven is keeping an eye out for us and cares for us to the extent that He promises to heal us. He promises to heal all of us who call upon Him sincerely.

We know from reading the Bible that these aren't empty promises. God fulfils all His promises and that's why we can be confident that His Word will come to pass.

> *So shall my word be that goeth forth out of my mouth: it shall not return unto me void, but it shall accomplish that which I please, and it shall prosper in the thing whereto I sent it.* (Isaiah 55:11)

According to the Scriptures 353 prophesies have been fulfilled in Jesus our Saviour. (See NOTES.)

> *For had ye believed Moses, ye would have believed me: for he wrote of me.* (John 5:46)

RESTORATION OF HEALTH

GOD SHALL WIPE AWAY ALL *tears* FROM THEIR EYES; AND THERE SHALL BE NO MORE *DEATH*, NEITHER *SORROW*, NOR *CRYING*, NEITHER SHALL THERE BE ANY MORE *PAIN*...

REVELATION 21:4

VERSE 24 - GOD SHALL WIPE AWAY ALL TEARS FROM THEIR EYES; AND THERE SHALL BE NO MORE DEATH, NEITHER SORROW, NOR CRYING, NEITHER SHALL THERE BE ANY MORE PAIN...

Some people say that these promises are made for the afterlife, and that's reassuring and no doubt true, but I didn't know anything much about the afterlife when I read these words. I simply understood that I would be comforted in this life, as indeed I have been.

Is my life now a bed of roses? Uh... no. But I feel extraordinarily loved and cared for, and daily experience improvements in all areas of my life and a joy I never dreamed was possible.

I have progressed on from lying in bed all day in a darkened room to now spending most of my time on my recliner in the living room.

From not being able to do anything much at all, over the last couple of years I have been able, with help from many people, to build my gift shop and my free Scripture card website. This means that others can benefit from Scripture as I did, and enjoy these wonderful Scripture verses and send them to friends and family for free.

With the help of Self-Publishing School and the support of fellow students I have been able to publish two bestsellers so far, and the book you're reading now, *God Healed Me,* is my third one. (See NOTES.)

If any upsets or upheavals happen, as inevitably they do in this earthly life for all of us, my faith and GOD's Word provide healing. It is Scripture verses such as those which are found in this book that help me through rough times.

There failed not ought of any good thing which the Lord had spoken... all came to pass. (Joshua 21:45)

GOD WIPES AWAY ALL TEARS

AFTERWORD

WITH GOD ON YOUR SIDE ALL THINGS ARE POSSIBLE.

The prophet Moses, who lived around 1400 BC, was chosen by GOD to save his people from slavery in Egypt.

Moses refused to go to Pharaoh and tell him to let the people go. One of the reasons Moses gave GOD for not being able to do as GOD asked him to was that Moses wasn't a very good speaker.

To this GOD responded that he made all, including the dumb, the deaf, the seeing, and the blind. So don't think for a moment that experiencing disability and illness may not be part of God's plan, or that this is your 'fault' or 'punishment.'

And then GOD said, *"Go, I'll be with you and teach you what to say."*

Moses said unto the Lord,

> *O my Lord, I am not eloquent... but I am slow of speech, and of a slow tongue.*

And the Lord said unto him,

> *Who hath made man's mouth? Or who maketh the dumb, or deaf, or the seeing, or the blind? Have not I, the Lord? Now therefore go, and I will be with thy mouth, and teach thee what thou shalt say.* (Exodus 4:10-15)

How is that? Having an impediment of some kind, or being disabled in some way, does not give anyone an excuse to not perform their duty or calling in life.

GOD clearly said to whatever Moses brought up as an excuse, *'I'll take care of it, just do as I tell you.'*

The upshot was that Moses' brother became his spokesperson and as we know, the rest is history; the Hebrew people were rescued from slavery and grew into a mighty nation as had been prophesied.

When God asked Moses to do something. Moses threw up all kinds of excuses, including physical impairment, as reasons for not rising up to the task.

GOD removed all obstacles and Moses eventually, albeit with modifications, did as he was told.

This historical event of around 3,500 years ago shows me that whatever my physical disabilities are, GOD may decide to use me for some task, and I better show up, brush up, and measure up.

Fears and disabilities are no excuse for not living out our dreams and fulfilling our destiny. With GOD on our side, all things are possible.

> *'Do not fear, for I am with you; do not be dismayed, for I am your God. I will strengthen you and help you; I will uphold you with my righteous right hand...*
>
> *The LORD is with me; I will not be afraid. What can mere mortals do to me?* (Isaiah 41:10, Psalm 118:6)

Fear not, GOD is with you, if you want Him to be. He promises to be there for us when we call upon Him. Isn't that just awesome?

> *He shall call upon me, and I will answer him: I will be with him in trouble; I will deliver him, and honour him.* (Psalm 91:15)

I pray for good health for all my readers and enough faith to move mountains.

Mimi

NOTES

Ask and it shall be given you.

Within a day of reciting this Scripture verse, I received a cheque for $15,000. as I recall on my WordPress blog. https://liveforeverhowto.wordpress.com/2014/11/21/with-god-all-things-are-possible-true-story/

The Power of Prayer

In the most widely publicized studies of the effect of intercessory prayer, cardiologist Randolph Byrd studied 393 patients admitted to the coronary-care unit at San Francisco General Hospital. Some were prayed for by home-prayer groups, others were not. The results were dramatic and surprised many scientists.

Prayer works!

Dr. Matthews cites studies suggesting that people who pray are less likely to get sick, are more likely to recover from surgery and illness, and are better able to cope with their illnesses than people who don't pray.
http://www.newsmax.com/Health/Headline/prayer-health-faith-medicine/2015/03/31/id/635623/ and
http://1stholistic.com/prayer/hol_prayer_proof.htm

Successful Prayer Formula

'Knock and it shall be opened to you.' For our prayers to be answered, we have to play our part. I address this on my WordPress blog 'LiveForeverHowTo' when I discuss Scripture card 'K.'
https://liveforeverhowto.wordpress.com/2015/05/04/free-scripture-card-k-knock-and-it-shall-be-opened-unto-you-there-is-a-minimum-of-sixteen-parts-to-this-formula/

God Hears Prayer

'God Hears Prayer' song with Pat Lewis from 103rd Street Gospel Choir. https://amzn.com/B001NMXF6U.

Raise me up, please!

In *My Story of Survival* I explain how I prayed to 'be raised up' without having much of an understanding what this meant. And I was 'raised up' in the most humorous way... touching the ceiling, as the physicians walked in. http://amzn.com/B018QDEKXK.

Survey on Prayer

Survey on prayer from Belief.net:
http://www.beliefnet.com/Faiths/Faith-Tools/Meditation/2004/12/U-S-News-Beliefnet-Prayer-Survey-Results.aspx

353 fulfilled prophesies

According to the Scriptures 353 prophesies have been fulfilled in Jesus our Saviour.

http://www.accordingtothescriptures.org/prophecy/353propheci es.html

OTHER BOOKS BY MIMI EMMANUEL

My Story of Survival

My Story of Survival became a bestseller in over 10 categories within weeks of launching. *My Story of Survival* contains a ten-ingredient-only diet with oodles of faith, and also the ultimate low-reactive diet for allergies, gut problems, food intolerances, and chemical sensitivities. http://amzn.com/B018QDEKXK.

Mimi's Book Launch Plan

Mimi's Book Launch Plan, another bestseller listed as such in 8 categories at Amazon, outlines how to launch your e-book easy peasy, with diary notes of a 31-day countdown and to-do overview. http://amzn.com/B01BU0VV1A.

Glimpses of Light anthology

Mimi also contributed to the anthology *Glimpses of Light*. During 2015, the International Year of Light, twenty-one authors from Australia and the United States came together to explore the theme of 'glimpses of light' — finding light in dark places — through short stories, poems, flash fiction, and creative non-fiction. By Jeanette O'Hagan, Nola Passmore, et al. http://amzn.com/B019FLDHHM.

Like A Girl anthology

Like a Girl is another anthology Mimi contributed to. Fourteen authors from around the world wrote stories to raise money for PLAN Australia, supporting girl's education. By Mirren Hogan, et al. http://amzn.com/B018WMRMFS.

PROMOS, FREE BOOKS AND FREEBIES

Coming up are 'LIVE FOREVER HOW TO' and 'THE HOLY GRAIL OF BOOK LAUNCHING.'

To receive a copy of my next book for FREE, sign up to Mimi's Book Releases. Here http://eepurl.com/bHUzf5

If you enjoyed 'GOD HEALED ME,' please consider leaving a review on Amazon. This is how others readers can also find this book.

To talk to me, place bulk orders or if you have suggestions for improvements, I'd love to hear from you at mimi@mimiemmanuel.com.

I recommend that all my readers read the full story.

For the full story grab yourself a Bible.

Visit www.freescripturecards.com to send
free Scripture cards to your friends and family.

Visit www.mosaichouse.co to order
hardcopy Scripture Cards on healing.

Visit http://eepurl.com/b5q_OP
to download your FREE Scripture cards.

Thank you for respecting the copyright (©myemmanuel2015) on
these designs and only utillising the Scripture Cards for your own
personal use.

Printed in Great
Britain
by Amazon